# The Cigar Box Poems

## Christine Brooks

Clare Songbirds Publishing House Poetry Series
ISBN 978-1-947653-84-9
Clare Songbirds Publishing House
*The Cigar Box Poems* © 2020 Christine Brooks

All Rights Reserved. Permission to reprint individual poems must be obtained from the author who owns the copyright.

Printed in the United States of America
FIRST EDITION

**Clare Songbirds Publishing House Mission Statement:**
Clare Songbirds Publishing House was established to provide a print forum for the creation of limited edition, fine art from poets and writers, both established and emerging. We strive to reignite and continue a tradition of quality, accessible literary arts to the national and international community of writers, and readers. Chapbook manuscripts are carefully chosen for their ability to propel the expansion of art and ideas in literary form. We provide an accessible way to promote the art of words in order to resonate with, and impact, readers not yet familiar with the siren song of poets and writers. Clare Songbirds Publishing House espouses a singular cultural development where poetry creates community and becomes commonplace in public places.

140 Cottage Street
Auburn, New York 13021
www.claresongbirdspub.com

# Contents

| | |
|---|---:|
| War | 9 |
| Lauds | 10 |
| Impeachment Day | 12 |
| The Man | 13 |
| The Monarch | 14 |
| Shadows | 15 |
| Father Time | 16 |
| Centipede | 18 |
| Sister | 19 |
| Shattered | 20 |
| Puff | 21 |
| Grapes | 22 |
| The Writer | 23 |
| Ugly Girl | 24 |
| Autumn's Breath | 26 |
| I Had No Idea | 27 |
| The Moments | 28 |
| Two Dead Mothers | 29 |
| Crucifixion Street | 30 |
| The Kite | 32 |
| Cocktails with Dad | 33 |
| 5 | 35 |
| The Runner | 36 |
| Chasing Ghosts | 38 |
| The Cigar Box | 40 |
| Emily | 41 |
| White   Space | 42 |

| | |
|---|---|
| Alive | 43 |
| Brother | 44 |
| Two Dead Soldiers | 45 |
| The Fat Seagull | 46 |
| Dorian | 47 |
| White Noise | 48 |
| Youth | 49 |

The author wishes to thank the publications in which poems in this collection have previously appeared.

*Door Is a Jar*, Issue 7, Spring 2018 "The Ugly Five poems"
*The Cabinet of Heed*, Issue 9, 2018, "The Writer"
*Riggwelter Press*, December 2018 "Finding God"
*peculiars magazine*, 2018, "Shattered"
*The Mystic Blue Review*, 5th Issue "Puff," "Sisters," "Grapes"
*Gazing Grain Press,* "Small Packages" 2018 Semi Finalist
*Amethyst Review,* "The Monarch," October 2018, "The Man," November 2018
*The Vessel Press*, "Lauds," 2018
Collective Unrest, "Impeachment Day," January 2019
*Twist in Time Magazine*, "Father Time" December 2019
*Brave Voices Magazine*, "Emily," January 2019

*To Sister Karol,
Mentor,
Spiritual advisor,
Weirdest sister,
Friend*

## *War*

The neglected bacon, now too crunchy for her,
spat out in shards
as she mumbles something.
Pass the eggs.
Pretty please
I say, sitting up straight and smiling
at my reflection in the curio cabinet behind her.
Dad salts and peppers.
Using the mismatched knife and fork violently
chopping up, his over hard eggs.
More bacon, he says loudly
laughing at a joke he heard earlier at the bar down the street
startling me. I spill my orange juice. My shaking hands quickly
wipe it up with the torn paper towel.
Sorry.
Sorry.
Salting and peppering and taking big gulps of his milk
Mom passes the heaping plate of burned slabs of meat that look more like
dead soldiers stacked up
than dinner.
All I hear is his cutting. Cutting of eggs. Cutting of toast.
Attacking each bite as if he had not eaten in days.
Mumble mumble. I dodge the shrapnel.
She says nothing.
The clock strikes seven.

### *Lauds (Morning Prayer)*

I feel you here
in this stone house of old souls & silent reflection
floating,
mixing with the
Frankincense and white roses.

Our spirits, faint gold
mingle, touch, become one
ever briefly.

Unseen dancers
Together again
Together at last.

I want to stay here, to be with you
heavy, peaceful, forever and forever
but I cannot.

There is so much to see
so much, still, to do.

As the bell tolls eleven
waking me from my thoughts,
you return to the place of unremembered dreams,
that I can only visit

When my heart is full,
and the window to my soul,
Open.

I reach out to you, one last time
across the misty cool divide,
but you have gone ahead
again
leaving me alone in this sacred space,
this holy place.

It is only my face now, that looks back at me
through the slants of stained glass
and only the sound of my heartbeat that I hear.

I will see you again my friend,
when my path rises up
to meet yours
in the house of tomorrows
where we will once again,
dance and laugh &
sing.


Oh the stories I will tell.
Oh the love I will have.
Oh the love.
Oh the love.

## *Impeachment Day*

He's ugly,
stand behind me child. You're safe now but — look away.
But,
I want to see him.
He is hideous. He has horns and a forked tail and
holes where his eyes should be.
Beauty is on the inside, I say to the back of her front.

No. Not this time. His heart is ugly, his words hurtful
and his language vulgar.
There must be good in him.
Everyone has some good.
Not him. Now hush.

But I can't see. Or talk.
Please.

I'll describe it to you.

Lift me up.

You said, they are all monsters.
He is the worst because he looks like the
monster they all are.

Lift me up, please
So I can see the revolution.

Ssshhhh.

## *The Man*

Who does he pray for?
This older man who, unafraid
walks to the front of the church
kneels,
praying, as it appeared he had
every day, for many days.
Perhaps, many years.

Had his wife gone ahead without him?
Had a dear friend been lost?
Perhaps his own soul had
been broken, battered, in need of absolution?

I could not ask, to do so would violate the quiet holy place.
As he teetered and tottered,
slowly rising from the hard tile alter
he glanced at me.

For one moment, we were connected, two sinners
recognizing each other, for one cosmic instant
not measured on any clock,
we were
one.

### *The Monarch*

He floated in, as if he had been here before, as if,
strangely,
he knew his way.

He stayed, moments only, perhaps,
strong in the warm summer breeze,
confidant
of his ability to fly away at any time,
allowing me in,
ever briefly.

Dancing the fragile dance,
that afternoon
both strong apart —
Fragile,
together.

He fluttered, opening his strong wings emblazoned with bold
orange and black so dark it appeared blue

Powerful,
gentle,
until the moment his colors
burst into flame,
and he was gone,
leaving only his imprint
on my soul.

## *Shadows*

We visited
    last night
I saw her there, sitting
on the edge of the blue couch
smiling gently, but wringing her porcelain hands,
and looking
  restless,
smooth knotty walking stick by her side,
never saying a word.

It was different this time
This time she was real.
This time she was here.
This time she was
really here.

This time, though
she knew she was dead
and so did I.

I went to her anyway, slowly
even in death,
but she faded to ash
as I reached out,
vanishing completely,
reminding me again,
that she is here, but
I am
alone.

## *Father Time*

t
i
c
k

t
o
c
k


The grandfather
clock, keeps
time, twelve
gongs. She
has made
it to another day.

Silence, outside the
dining room window
where she lay
dying. Darkness shrouds
the small house that
holds her body, while
her soul prepares for flight.

Tick tock. The grand clock just won't stop
TICKING
If only it would, she could stay. The chime builds now,
at quarter past the hour. I wish I could hold the hands
of Father Time. Hold them tight, so they could not move, could
not take her to the place I cannot visit.

The silence is pierced by the crunch of a slow-moving car on
the ice. Where are they going at this late hour? Tick tock. The
pressure is mounting. The chime ever building on the grand
clock, as it reminds me with every tick and every tock that
the night is fading, time is winning. And I am not in charge.
Stop! Stop! I yell to the fucking clock. But it is deaf to my
pleas, and just keeps marching on to the Valley of Death,
playing its death march tick tock tick tock.

Half past the hour now the chime is louder, longer now taunting me. I hold her close stroke her arm. Remove the cool facecloth from her forehead. It won't help her anymore. His arms are around her now. So I know it is time to let go. The clock has stopped no more tick no more tock. Grief takes time they say but how can I heal when the clock has gone silent?

*Centipede*

I caught a clear centipede
as it scampered by
to save it from their heavy boots

Safely, carefully
I set it free out the window of my
third floor office

It was only later that I realized
centipedes cannot
fly.

***Sister***

Blood is thicker
than water, but it doesn't
matter
when her veins pulse with
oil.

## *Shattered*

Sometimes, a flame
is not a flame — at all.
Sometimes, it is glass
that shatters
leaving only darkness & questions in the place that was once
light.

## *Puff*

I spent twenty minutes watching a dandelion puff dance and
flutter to music I could not hear.

It soared far up, deep into the gangly wooden arms of the grand
American Yellowwood tree
only to gently fall

   side to side

Floating peacefully unaware that
it must land.
It was as if the pilot of that puff
knew that its journey was short in time so it must be long in
experience.

Each time it neared the damp earth and certain death, a gentle
breeze would capture it
and blow it back to the heavens.

This magical dance continued
until finally, a blade of wet grass
slightly taller than the others, contacted the fragile traveler,
causing it to stop
being a puff, and begin being
a memory.

## *Grapes*

They call to me
from their twisted branches
come blossom with me

in the sun
and tell me a story.


I am only a toddler, they whisper
my trunk gets stronger every day
and my roots dig deeper and wider into the loose soil
as I stretch across the vast vineyard.


Soon my buds will break and my sap will rise
and my flowers will be perfectly, perfect.
My berries will change from green to
yellow, pink, red & purple.


I am beautifully alone
caring for myself,
but wishing for a gentle soul to sit with me
and tell me a story.


On quiet nights, with only the moon as company,
I pour a glass of their dark red friendship
and begin my story, that only they can hear.

It is,
the story of life, and it begins with a
   whisper.

## *The Writer*

I have poured the wine, skipped
the water,
Smoked the weed, and turned up the tunes in my headphones
Jackson Brown, Willie Nelson and — Miles Davis.

I have opened the window to my soul,
my empty space and let the cold in.
With the draft, the monsters come. At first, just a breeze,
a whisper and a damp breath on my warm neck.

I stare at their invited but unwelcome faceless faces,
see their hole
and grab hold of their hand.

Tight.

Sometimes, it is me dragging them to the place of no return
other times they grab hold of my warmth
with their death grip, pulling me down the
gravel-y path
upright and unafraid
towards the end where I trust they will push me,
holding on to the last thread of my essence
giving me a glimpse of the place that I cannot return from
so, I can face the abyss long enough to hear Its cry,
Its reasons, and Its story.


I trust the monsters to show me the face of Hell and Heaven
to let me take notes and return to tell Their tale.

Their story is interesting, so I return more often than I should,
the sirens call and I answer
over and over and over again
Until the day I do not return
again.

## *Ugly Girl*

Look at you,
hand me down clothes,
silly sneakers, and
Who cuts your hair?
Ugly girl.

I can't play with you anymore
You're adopted. I don't play with
adopted people.
That's what my mother said as she rang the dinner bell,
and said you have to go home
Ugly girl.

I can't do this assignment, I don't know my
genetics. Oh, just make it up. It doesn't matter anyways.
Not really.
I would not, make them up. I would guess, and that was
different.

Just put your finger on the fan blade, we'll be blood sisters
since we're not really sisters.
But it hurts, and it's bleeding
ALOT
It will scar, what's one more anyways? Don't be such a baby
Ugly girl.

Write down your family history
the stark white nurse says.
Oh, you can't? Ok we'll draw a big X through your history.
I would prefer it if you just leave it
blank, not crossed out.
Why are you being so difficult?
It really doesn't matter
Ugly girl.

And so, the ugly girl came to believe that ugly meant different,
having battle scars, and fortitude.
She came to believe that ugly meant brave and resilient. She
embraced her inner ugly, and marched onward, rarely questioning
her uniqueness, or the fact that she was often marching alone.

Still though on nights when there was no moon, she would look up at the dark night sky and wonder about her mother. She wondered why she gave her away, and if she knew how far she had come. She wondered if she ever thought of her, or had ever seen her. She wondered if she talked to the dark night sky too, or the thin blue line or anyone for that matter, that might be listening to her wishes and dreams.

Mostly though, she wondered if she was an ugly girl too.

## *Autumn's Breath*

The bright leaves
are slowly, dying
slowly turning from bright oranges & brilliant reds,
to burnt, dried rust colored
wisps of what they once were.
Their time? A season,
but they are only remembered
as they light up the sky one last time, before they are shaken
from her arms by autumn's cold breath, before the others
and fall with beauty, grace and joy.
The tree cannot hold them.
As her gangly wooden arm stretch far and wide,
empty now,
she is reminded that she is alone.

## *I Had No Idea*


There is another woman
with your same name,
who is your age, and lives nearby.

I had no feeling for her.

I wrote to her, twice
but she never replied.
Bitch,
I thought to myself. I was giving her another chance, rejecting
me was not something I planned for.
I had no tools to cope with her rejection. Again.
Something was off though, I had no feeling for her, and her
dismissal didn't exactly
hurt.

I had no idea what to do.

I began writing letters,
to Emily Dickinson, because I knew she was listening. I knew
my simple words, simple letters would unlock the door & show
me the way. You, could not write back, but
she
did,
many years ago, in a book that contains your family tree. Our
family tree. She left the clues.

I had no idea she was dead.

She died in her sleep of a heart attack, before she could even
retire. She would have tried to find me then, when she had time
and life was done beating her down. She would have done that.
I had no idea she was out there, thinking of me, as I, was thinking
of her. I had no idea I would finally find her, and have to make
peace with her spiritual self. I guess she will teach me to speak,
so she can hear me in the place she dwells that I can only visit
in my dreams.

I had no idea.

## *The Moments*

I wonder, how long you sat with me, telling me everything
would be alright,
stroking my cheek
touching my face.
looking into my eyes.
Did you cry, I wonder, or did I?
Did you feel a great sense of relief when you left me, or did
your heart shatter a million times over?
Did you say a prayer for me, or
sing me a song, or tell me you
loved me?
Did you try to breathe me in before you put me down, never to
be held again by you?
How long did it take?
I wonder,
for you to spend a lifetime with me?

## *Two Dead Mothers*

Floating
aimlessly but not without
purpose.
Drifting ever farther away from the safety of the shores. Away from the oyster bar, away from the beach bar, away from my spot in the sand, and away from everything familiar.
That's how it feels to ask questions you know you shouldn't ask, because somewhere deep down you already know the answers.

Drifting
waiting, watching for
Mother Nature to deliver you to
safety. A nice gentle ride. That's all, you ask.
A return to shore without loss of life, that's all. Simple.

Shore is calling.

The waves are brewing now, boiling over but still I wait, patiently, for the set to unfold. For Her to play her cards.

Paddling
Now I haven't decided to get after it. Dive in and take it on head first. All or nothing, live or die.
It's turbulent all around, every direction of Mother is pulling, tugging and pushing me to make a decision. Dig deeper into the dark unknown or swim for shore.
Safety.

Two shadows, pulling
this way and that. Sirens calling
Dark clouds push me away,
push me towards safety but
still, something deep inside me dreams of, the outside.
The place just beyond the break.
That's how it feels,
to have two dead mothers.

## *Crucifixion Street*

Dear Cynthia,
I found him
my brother
even though he didn't make it easy for me
I looked everywhere
only to find, on some level
him
searching for me.

My whole life I dreamed of seeing my face, my eyes,
and my lips on someone else
and now I have.
We have not met
only through emails and
pictures, have we gotten to know each other.

He scares me,
his father scares me, and even though he says he isn't mine,
I think, maybe, that he is.
You named me after your mother,
Monica.
You wanted to keep me.

I think that man did something,
something terrible, so
you hid me away.
I held the only key.

My brother, your son, has issues you knew of,
and the old man sits in prison
for the rest of his life.
You did for me what any good mother would; you protected
me, never revealing my identity
Ever.
I saw your grave, and found small comfort in knowing you
once stood in the same place
when your parents died.
You looked at the same mountains, the same trees,
and I wonder, did you think of me?

I have carried a heavy cross
of pain and rejection
for a lifetime.

Now it is time to rest

to forgive
and to get to know you
on
Crucifixion Street

***The Kite***

The kite

so frail & thin

flies high among the

great winds, ripped and

torn, fearless, she flies higher

still. The fiercer the gust, still she rises

until the time comes that she has given all of herself,
and there is nothing left but the

string that like an arrow, gave her life.

## *Cocktails with Dad*

I can get my original birth certificate now.
Don't tell me.
But I want you to be part of my life, this new chapter.
Don't tell me.
He would say
Over and over
Which only made me feel like
more of a liar
more of a betrayer
Judas.

Being born gave me a little of all of those.
Birth alone provided me with a crime
without alibi.

A few more Bud Lites for him
Yes
More wine for me, yes.
But no
even more adamant
PLEASE
don't tell me.
Covering his ears.
Ok.

I hate secrets.
I am not built for lies. My house
of cards, while wobbly, is built
on the wobbly truth,
not the steadfastness of a lie.

Here's a chip
and another
Drinks all around.
Cheer for everyone.
Don't tell me anymore.
Let's dance.
Please
Let's just dance.

## 5

pure white,
secluded, strange,
Union News, father's house,
letters, unrequited love
death of mother.

starch white, life happens
all over us, all the time
staining
ever slightly
the perfect immaculate envelope.

pearly white, streaks of platinum
less bright, but still
shining, others will notice
still,
that they are strange.
bit by bit, white coals
turn to ash.

embers now, being fanned
secluded, strange,
Union News, father's house,
letters, unrequited love
death of mother.

## *The Runner*


As long as I can remember,
It chased me.
It followed me,
It knew my hiding places even before I did, and
It never stopped hunting me.

For over four decades, It has come after me
night after night
waiting for peace to settle in,
waiting, always patiently, for me to let happiness distract me,
and for the right moment
to begin its endless pursuit
off guard but never surprised,
I run.

Knowing it will check all my
secret places, I know I cannot
linger in safety too long.

First the bushes, always the bushes across from a church
that I do not know,
I hide. Looking. Waiting
for a break, a chance to run again.

Down a city block,
exposed, I stay close to the building.
It is close now,
I cannot see It, but I feel Its evil pant,
breathing down my neck
hairs on end, goose bumps now,
I must run.

I won't make it; my next spot is too far away. I must hide
now
in this place that I have never been, but that is familiar
danger is here, she is coming.
She wishes me no harm,
but It watches her, and she will lead It to me.

I run to the attic of a childhood home, momentary safety,
still, It knows where I am, It always knows.
I must run.

I want to face It,
see the ugly face of my nightmares, but my dream body will not
sacrifice its life for a mere
glimpse of
It.

I break through a door that had been boarded up
and land back on the street
    —alone.

It will end soon,
each night is the same,
I will wake up,
not as scared as I once was,
but still, each morning I will lie in my bed and wonder why
It chases me
Why it hunts me, and why It refuses to let me forget
what is best left un-remembered.

I pray to a God that I don't know listens, with prayers of peace
& forgiveness, but still
when I close my eyes, it will be waiting, tracking me,
until daybreak,
when I can rest, away from the darkness of my nightmares,
where evil hides in the shadows,
and safety lives in fleeting moments of solitude.

### *Chasing Ghosts*


I met her there
on Crucifixion Street, where the road bends slightly,
and an old Maple tree stands
guard.

I met her there, for the
first time
on a day in October that was
warmer than usual
wearing leggings, fleece lined flip flops, and a crisp white hoodie
I met her.

Off in the distance,
Mount Nonotuck
watched
over
as I said my first hello,
told her all about my life, and the person I had become,
all the while,
she remained quiet,
listening.

In this
sacred
place
I found her
resting peacefully.

I had been looking for her, for
decades
a lifetime, really.
Before I even knew I was searching, I was
listening, and looking
for her familiar face.

The leaves splashed with
reds & oranges
lay on the ground,
given life only by the
gentle
warm winds.

I met her there, the woman who gave me life,
the woman who gave me strength,
strength enough to be sent out
into the big world
alone.
Strength to
survive.

Where the road bends slightly
under an old Maple tree
ten grave stones in,
and five over,
I met my mother for the
first time.
I sipped warm apple cider
said a prayer, laid a small
white
seashell down on her stone,
and introduced myself.

Hello Cynthia,
I am your
daughter.

Thank you.

## *The Cigar Box*

In the broken-down cigar box, with a wobbly tattered lid
labeled with the neatness of a six year old - R O C K S  E T C.
Lie a shiny silver badge from my Papa
a reminder that in darkness, there is safety
a laminated military ID from my Popie, to remind me that danger hides in broad daylight,
sits next to it.

scattered about,
buttons from old cardigans and housecoats
remind me that what holds us together, exists also,
    independently

*Emily*

I wish I could pluck
  the roses,
off the wallpaper
and give
you a bouquet of
todays, bound
together with
 the threads of
tomorrows.

*White   Space*


   The purple roses breathe in,
and out,
my breath, in time,
as your bedroom walls
inhale — gently, softly, now
  with me

Exhaling, deeply, soulfully
in the place your spirit
 dwells.

I am there
carried on their
essence


You —

   are here.

*Alive*

The spider, so
real in my mind's eye,
creeping, crawling along
  my forearm,
a twitch,
both here and
   there
making the spider,
real, on
both planes,
  real and dream worlds melt,
 together
if only for a
  t w i t c h.

***Brother***

I met him there,
 by the grave

We didn't know then

   that
we visited the same
   mother.

***Two Dead Soldiers***

The clanking of the two empty beer bottles, leftover from Farm Aid
as they rolled around the
trunk, sounded more
like applause, then
sadness
of shells looking, wanting, to be full,
but instead, only together
drumming out,
 a lifeline

## *The Fat Seagull*

Fat, wet, angry
he toddled, and teetered, unsteady,
scavenging off bits of bone
   & shell
that had long ago given
their life, to his sharp yellow
bill & empty
black
eyes.

***Dorian***

My memory of

  you

 never ages

## *White Noise*

I want to cover my ears, I want to hum, or sing la la la loudly
over your words, your memories, your testimony.
I want to turn up Dylan,
Beatz blasting
Tremblin'
so, my mind doesn't hear your
thoughts, your recollections,
your truth.

No
I want to scream, no.
I want to cry.
I want to die.
I want to unhear, unknow and un remember,
those terrible nights, more than one, more than two,
maybe even, more than three
when I could not scream, I could not talk, and could never
ever tell.

I want to change the channel,
block out the noise,
I want it all to stop,
like it did last time, when I
just pretended it never happened.

## *Youth*

A breeze, gentle
  —just learning,
new and
warm
how to be a
GREAT wind, cold &
unforgiving.

Too young to
howl, too young to
bite.

Just strong enough to
flicker the
flame,
dance the curtains, &
give the green clamped leaves a
sing song-y voice,
in the grand
Yellowwood.

Uncrumpled pages
fall,
flowers perfume
drifts, never lingering
as each breath brings us peace, and
memories
of youthful
love.

Christine Brooks is a graduate of Western New England University with her B.A. in Literature and her M.F.A. from Bay Path University in Creative Nonfiction. Her poem, *the price*, is in the October issue of The Cabinet of Heed and her poems, *life* and *I Don't Believe*, are in the fall issue of Door Is a Jar. Two poems, *friends* and *demons* are in the January 2020 issue of Cathexis Northwest Press and her poem, *communion*, is in the January 2020 issue of Pub House Books. Her series of vignettes, *Small Packages,* was named a semifinalist at Gazing Grain Press in August 2018. Her essay, *What I Learned from Being Accidentally Celibate for Five Years* was featured in HuffPost, MSN, Yahoo and Daily Mail UK in April 2019.

www.ingramcontent.com/pod-product-compliance
Lightning Source LLC
Chambersburg PA
CBHW030202100526
44592CB00009B/400